Python

An Ultimate Beginner's Guide to Python Programming

By Gale Gabon

The information herein is offered for informational purposes solely, and is universal as so. The presentation of the information is without contract or any type of guarantee assurance.

The trademarks that are used are without any consent, and the publication of the trademark is without permission or backing by the trademark owner. All trademarks and brands within this book are for clarifying purposes only and are the owned by the owners themselves, not affiliated with this document.

Executive Summary

During the last couple of decades, we've witnessed a significant growth in the number of programming languages—from the core dominant languages such as C, Fortran, COBOL in the 1960's and the 1970's to object-oriented C++, JavaScript, Java and Golang that we have today. In all these evolutions, Python programming language has stood out from the rest.

It's no secret that Python has continued to grow at a fast-paced rate, thanks to its open source nature. Besides, its ability to use succinct and easy-to-learn syntax—which makes it one of the most powerful and very flexible programming language—allows programmers to develop more complex software within a much shorter time compared to other programming languages.

So, why should you learn Python programming language? Truth be told—Python programming language is an excellent, easy-to-learn and super-powerful programming language that has ever been developed. As a matter of fact, the language has been used to power some of the most renowned websites applications such as the Google and the YouTube.

With several career options that require Python programming, learning Python can be a great asset to land your dream job! Also, you'll boost your career with new programming skills.

"An Ultimate Beginner's Guide to Python Programming" provides all the vital programming concepts and skills that you need to create your own software. The eBook will walk you through comprehensive step-by-step guidelines that are necessary to make you an efficient Python programmer. So, let's dive in.

Contents

Chapter 1: Getting started with Python

Welcome to Python programming. This section introduces you to the ins and outs of Python programming language. By the end of the chapter, you'll have a bigger picture view of everything that's required to succeed with Python programming.

Are you set to go?

Let's start with the most important question—how can you install Python?

How to install Python

The process of downloading and installing Python is generally easy. If you're using a recent Linux or UNIX distribution, then Python has already been installed on it. However, if you're using a Mac or Windows OS, then you'll be forced to download and install it on your own.

Before you download and install Python, you should decide on the version of Python that you should install. There are two versions of Python that you can use. These are Python 2 and Python 3. The version that you chose depends on the features that you'd like to have.

If you're using an environment that you can't control, then it's advisable to use version 2 as opposed to version 3 that allows you to use a free selection from other versions. On the other hand, Python 3 allows you to access more libraries. Besides, it eliminates many oddities that can hinder beginner programmers trying to learn Python.

Here's how you can download and install Python on Windows OS computers:

- Download the current version of Python that you'd like to use from the download site (Version 3.5.1 is the latest version).
- Open file that you've just downloaded to install.
- Accept the default settings from the on-screen instructions till your installation is completed.

Three approaches can be used with Python. These are:

- The **Python Shell**. It allows you to run the Python commands line by line.
- The **IDLE GUI**. It enables you to write more complex Python scripts and run them at once.
- The **Text Editor**. You can use any text editor that runs on your computer. However, you have to save the Python files using the ".py" extension and run them from the shell.

How can you launch Python?

On Windows OS platforms, launch Python by going to **Start>Programs** and clicking on the Python. If you have a Mac or a Linux system, then launch your terminal and then type "python." Now you're all set up to go.

Determine the approach you'd like to use when writing Python instructions (whether Python Shell, IDLE GUI or Text Editor). For illustration, I'll use the Python Shell approach.

Now follow these steps to write your first program:

- Open the Python Shell.
- Write the Python instructions in the shell.
- Hit the enter button.

That's it! It's really simple.

Here's a quick way to see the process in action .....Go ahead and copy / paste the code below into your Python Shell.

```
Print ("Hello World!")
```

The phrase "Hello World!" should appear.

Congratulations! You've written your first Python code. Don't bother soo much about what the statements mean for now. We'll explain the technical details in our succeeding chapters.

An Overview of Python Application

Now that you've run your first Python program, what next? You should now begin learning vital Python programming concepts and skills that are essential for you to create your own Python software.

But first, you should understand the structure of Python applications.

All Python programs have the following structure:

```
import sys

def main ():

main()

{

Program instructions

}
```

As you can note from the structure, all Python programs must start with the keyword *"import."* What's the significance of this statement?

Well, the primary reason why Python is considered a powerful programming language is that of its ability to handle a variety of tools for data management. However, none of the data management tools are available when Python starts up. These tools are defined in the modules that have to be loaded in Python using the import statement.

For instance, the statement below includes all the system libraries when executing Python programs:

```
import sys
```

Next up, let's explore names and namespaces in Python.

Whenever a Python program is loaded and run, the computer's memory always contains objects that contain function definitions. The function definitions help to place the function object into the computer's memory.

The objects in the memory can be specified with names. It's vital that objects are named during the creation time. Therefore, specifying the names makes object functions to be easily retrievable. For instance, the code below creates a function object and assigns it the name main:

```
def main ():
  if len (sys.argv) >= 4:
   name = sys.argv [2]
  else:
   name = "World"
  print ("Hello"), name
```

With the above definitions, the Python interpreter will execute all the function definitions in the Python file by placing a set of all the functions objects in memory and linking each of them with the namespace when the program is launched with the import statement.

So, there you have it—you've learned how to set up your and create your first application in Python.

Next up, we explore more about Python's variables and types.

Chapter 2: Variables and Types

Are you ready to learn about variables and types in Python? Fantastic. There are so many things that go on in the main memory whenever a Python program is being executed.

The program that you'll be developing in Python is simply a sequence of instructions that directs a computer to perform a particular task. Now, such an application must use data—which may include constants or variable values. If you can comprehend how data is managed in any programming language—Python included—then you'll be in a position to create robust, efficient and very powerful programs.

Well first, what exactly is a variable?

A variable can be viewed as a temporary storage location in the main memory. Put simply; a variable is a temporary storage area that holds data while your program is running. This implies that when you create a variable, you're actually reserving a space in the main memory to hold your data.

All the variables that you define should have a data type. If you've specified a data type for your variable, the Python interpreter will allocate the memory and decide what to store in the reserved memory space. Therefore, by assigning variables to data types, you can store numbers, characters, and constants in the main memory.

Being an oriented programming language, Python is not "statically typed." In Python, every variable that you define is an object. Therefore, you don't have to declare variables—and their types—before using them.

Python variables are usually are identified by names or identifiers. Just like other programming languages, the conventions for naming variables must strictly be adhered to. Here are some naming conventions that you should follow when creating variables in Python:

- All the variable names should always start with a letter or an underscore.
- Variable names cannot start with a number.
- Don't use the special symbols when naming the variables.
- Ensure the maximum number of characters for your variables doesn't exceed 255.

I know you're thinking, "How can I assign values to variables in Python?"

How to assign values to Variables in Python

To reserve a memory location, the variables you'll use in Python don't require explicit declaration. In other programming languages, you have to declare a variable explicitly before you assign a value to it. However, in Python, the declaration of variables occurs automatically the moment you assign a value to the variable.

We use the equal sign (=) to assign values to variables. For instance, the statement;

```
count=10
```

Automatically reserves a memory space called count and assigns 10 to it.

You can also assign a single value to several variables at the same time. For instance, the statement below reserves memory spaces for 2 variables namely: age and count and assigns them value 100:

```
age, count=100
```

Which data types are supported in Python?

Python has different data types that are used to define the storage methods and operations that are possible on each of them. Here are examples of the standard data types in Python:

- Numbers
- String
- List
- Tuple
- Dictionary

Let's examine these data types in detail.

#1: Numbers

The Number data types are used to store numeric values. The Number objects will automatically be created whenever you assign a value to the variable. For example, the Python code below creates 2 variable objects (age and count) and assigns them the values 10 and 100 respectively:

```
age = 10
count= 100
```

You can delete reference to the Number object by using the "del" keyword before the name of the variable. For instance, the code below deletes the objects age and count that had previously been reserved and assigned values:

```
del age, count
```

You may be wondering, "How does Python handle the different types of numbers?" Good question.

Well, Python supports four different number types. These are:

- int (signed integers). These include the whole numbers of varying sizes from 8 bits to 32 bits.
- Long. These are long integers that are represented either in octal and hexadecimal numbering notation.
- Float. These are floating real point values of different bit sizes.
- Complex. These are complex numbers.

Here's an example of how you can use number data types in Python:

```
myint = 7
print ("The Number I have just typed is an Integer: %d" % myint)
```

#2: Strings

The Python strings are stored as consecutive sets of characters. Python allows the programmer to use either pair of single or double quotes when defining strings. Other subsets of strings can be specified using slice operator ([ ] and the [:]) with the indexes that start from 0 at the beginning of the string.

The plus (+) operator is used for string concatenation while the asterisk (*) is used as the repetition operator. Here's an example of a Python code that uses Strings:

```
mystr = "This is a case of a string."

print mystr        # This statement will print the complete string

print mystr [0]      # this statement prints out the first character of
the string

print mystr [2:5]      # this statement prints characters beginning
from the third to the fifth

print mystr [3:]     # Prints string starting from the fourth character

print mystr * 2      # this statement prints the string two times

print mystr + "in Python" #this statement prints the concatenated
string
```

What do you think will be the output of the above Python code?

#3: Lists

Lists are similar to arrays in C programming language. However, Python lists may contain items that do not necessarily belonging to the same data type. The list includes items that are separated by commas and enclosed in the square brackets ([]). Lists are defined by providing their names and initializing them with values. The following is an example of how a list can be defined in Python:

```
myList = ["Jupiter", "Earth", "Mars", "Pluto", "Saturn"]
```

You can access the individual elements in a list in the same way you do for an array. For instance:

myList [0] is the first item in the list.

We can use the use the methods *"insert"*, *"append"* and **"extend"** to add elements to an existing list.

The insert method demands that the index and the value to be added to the list are known in advance. For instance, the Python code below illustrates how insert method can be used to insert an element in a list at index 2:

```
myList. insert (2, "Mercury")
```

The append method takes one or more data elements as an input and adds them to the existing list. Here's an example:

```
myList. Append (["Sun", "Moon"])
```

The other method used to add elements to an existing list is the extend method. Just like the append method, the extend method expects one or more values as an input. However, unlike the append method, all the data elements are added as individual elements. Here's an example:

```
myList.extend (["Stars", "Meteors"])
```

Python lists can easily be searched for the values using an index method. The index method should specify the value to be searched where the output is the index of the location where the value has been kept. Here is an example that searches for the element "Saturn" in myList:

```
myList.index ("Saturn")
```

The delete method is used to remove items from a list. Here is an example of Python code that removes an item "Saturn" from myList:

```
myList. Remove ("Saturn")
```

#4: Tuples

Python tuples contain a number of values that are separated by commas. But unlike the lists—where the elements and sizes can be changed—tuples must be enclosed within the parentheses and can't be updated. For example, the Python code below creates a tuple named "months_of_the_year":

```
Months_of_the_year                                          =
("Jan","Feb","Mar","Apr","May","June","July","Aug","Sept","Oct","
Nov","Dec")
```

Here's an example of Python code that demonstrates the use of tuples:

```
print months_of_the_year        # Prints the complete tuple

print months_of_the_year [0]     # Prints first element of the tuple

print months_of_the_year [1:3]    # Prints elements starting from
the second to the third

print months_of_the_year [2:]     # Prints elements that starting
from the third element

print months_of_the_year * 2   # Prints tuple two times

print  months_of_the_year  +  months_of_the_year  # Prints  the
concatenated tuple
```

#5: Dictionaries

The Python's dictionaries operate in a similar fashion to hash tables. Put simply, the Python dictionaries are basically associative arrays— or hashes—that consist of key-value pairs where the dictionary key can assume any Python data type. However, we usually use numbers or strings to define the dictionary keys. On the other hand, the dictionary values can assume an arbitrary Python object.

The Python Dictionaries are always enclosed by the curly brackets ({ }), and the values can be assigned and accessed using the square brackets ([]). Here's an example:

mydict = {}

mydict["One"] = "This is 1."

mydict[2]   = "This is 2"

smalldict = {"name": "Peter Namisiko", "code":722848386, "dept": "IT"}

Here's an example of how you can use Python Dictionaries:

```
print mydict["one"]     # Prints value for 'one' key

print mydict[2]        # Prints the value for 2 key

print smalldict        # Prints the complete dictionary

print smalldict.keys()   # Prints all the keys
```

We've come to the end of the chapter on variables and types. Remember, writing efficient Python programs expects you to master all the variables and data types. Use the right variables and data types to develop efficient Python programs.

Next up, we explore types and casting in Python programming.

Chapter 3: Types and Casting in Python

Typecasting allows programmers to alter an entity from one data type into another. You may be thinking, "Why do I need type casting in Python?"

Well, if you want to take advantage of certain properties of object data type hierarchies, then you'll be forced to change entities from one data type to another. For instance, if you have an integer data type, and you want this to be converted into floating numbers, you should cast such data types.

Now that you understand why type casting is important let's jump in and get started.

To convert between the different types, you'll use the data type name as the function. Several built-in functions can help you to convert from one data type to another. These functions will always return a new object that represents the converted value.

Here are examples of those functions:

- int(x [,base]). It converts the value x to an integer where the base defines if x is a string or not.
- long(x [,base]). It converts the value x to the long integer where the base specifies if x is a string or not.
- float(x). It converts the value x to a floating-point number.
- complex (real [,imag]). It generates a complex number.
- str(x). It converts the object x to string representations.
- repr(x). It converts the object x to the expression string.
- eval(str). It evaluates the string and returns the object.
- tuple(x). It converts the value x to a tuple.
- list(x). It converts the value x to a list.
- set(x). It converts the value x to a set.

- dict(x). It converts the value x to a dictionary where x must be a sequence of the (key, value) tuples.
- chr(x). It converts the integer to a character.
- unichr(x). It converts an integer to the Unicode character.
- ord(x). It converts the single character to its integer value.
- hex(x). It converts an integer to a hexadecimal string.
- oct(x). It converts an integer to an octal string.

Take a look at the example of the code below. What do you think will be the output of the code?

```
x = "1000"

y = "-950"

print (x + y)

print int(x) + int(y)
```

The output of the above code will be:

```
1000-950

50
```

Can you explain why the output is like that?

Well, there you have it. You should now be in a position to begin converting from data type to another in Python.

Chapter 4: Python's Basic Programming Operators

Programming Operators are symbols that help to tell the Python interpreter to perform specific operations. Some of these operations may be mathematical, relational or even logical. The Python programming interpreter has a rich in built-in operators. These operators can be grouped into:

- Arithmetic Operators
- Relational Operators
- Logical Operators
- Bitwise Operators
- Assignment Operators

Without further ado, let's jump in and explore these operators.

#1: Arithmetic Operators

These are operators that are used for arithmetic operations. Below are examples of Python's arithmetic operators and their functions:

- +. It is used to add two operands. For instance, if A=100 and B=200 then A+ gives 300 as the answer.
- -. It is used to subtract the second operand from the first operand. For example, if A=20 0 and B=150 then A - B will yield 50 as the answer.
- *. It multiplies two or more operands. For example, if A=100 and B=200 then A*B produces 2000.
- /. It's used for division purposes. For instance, if A=100 and B=200 then, A/B produces 0.5.
- %. It is the modulus operator (it displays the remainder of a number after performing an integer division). For instance, if A=8 and B=3, then A % B yields 2 as a remainder.
- ++. It is the increment operator (it increases an integer value by one). For instance, if A=200, then A++ produces 201.
- - -. It is the decrement operator. For example, if A=200, then A- - produces 199.

#2: Relational Operators

Relational operators are used for comparison purposes. Below are examples of relational operators and their functions:

- ==. It verifies whether the values of the two operands are equal or not. If they are equal, then condition becomes true otherwise the condition is false. For instance, A==B is only true if A=200 and B=200.
- !=. It verifies whether the values of the two operands are equal or not. For instance, A! =B is false if A=200 and B=200.
- >. It checks whether the value of the left operand is greater than the value of the operand on the right-hand side.
- <. It checks whether the value of the left operand is less than the value of the operand on the right-hand side.
- >=. It checks whether the value of the left operand is greater than or equal to the value of the operand on the right-hand side.
- <=.It checks whether the value of the left operand is less than or equal to the value of the operand on the right-hand side.

#3: Logical Operators

Below are examples of logical operators and their functions:

- &&. It's called the logical AND operator. If both the operands are not zero, then the condition is true. Otherwise, the condition is false.
- ||. It's called the logical OR operator. If any of two operands is not zero, then output is true.
- !. It's called the Logical NOT Operator. It reverses the logical state of its initial operand.

#4: Bitwise Operators

The bitwise operators are used to perform bit-by-bit operations in Python programming. Below are examples of Python's bitwise operators and their functions:

- &. It's called the binary AND operator. It is used to copy a bit to the result if it exists in both the operands.
- |. It's called the binary OR operator. It is used to copy a bit if it exists in either of the operands.
- ^. It is called the binary XOR operator. It is used to copy the bit if it is set in only one operand and not both operators.
- <<. It is called the binary left shift operator. It is used to move the left side by a number of bits that are specified by the right operand.
- >>. It's called the binary right shift operator. It is used to move the right side by some bits that are specified by the right operand.

#5: Assignment Operators

Below are examples of assignment operators and their uses:

- =. It assigns values of the right side operands to the left side operand.
- +=. It is used to add the right operand to left operand and assign the output to the left operand.
- -=. It is used to subtract the right operand to left operand and assign the output to the left operand.
- *=. It is used to multiply the right operand and left operand and assign the output to the left operand.
- /=. It is used to divide the right operand and left operand and assign the output to the left operand.

Ready for your first test? Good. Here you go:

Open the Shell and copy the Python code below, making sure to include every letter and symbol, correctly. When you're done, press the Enter key to execute the file.

Python Code:

```
import sys

def main ():

main()

{

a = 5

d = 5

b = "This Program demonstrates Python Operators."

e = "This Program demonstrates Python Operators."

c = [1,2,3]

f = [1,2,3]

print(a is not d)

print(b is e)

print(c is f)

}
```

What do you see?

Here is one more test.

Python code:

```
m = 10

n= 12

print("m > n  is", m>n)

print("m < n  is", m<n)

print("m == n is", m==n)

print("m != n is",m!=n)

print("m >= n is",m>=n)

print("m <= n is",m<=n)
```

We've come to the end of operators. You're on your way to becoming a Python guru! Keep up the good work.

Chapter 5: Decision Making and Repetition Structures

Decision making in any programming language is absolutely necessary. They not only allow your program to arrive at decisions—which are based on user inputs or the results a processing action—but also help to control the flow of your program.

The decisions that help to control the flow of your program will be based on principles of logic and relational mathematical operators. For instance, you may want to compare two or more variables to determine the largest between the two. In this instance, you have to use logical and relational mathematical operators to help you control the flow of the Python program.

On the other hand, the repetition structures help a programmer to specify processes or instructions that are repeated—or iterated—until some condition is met. The advantages of repetition structures are two-fold. First, they'll enable you to use your variables in an efficient manner. Second, they can help you to organize statements that must be repeated for a block so long as a specific condition has been met.

So, which are the decision making and repetition structures in Python?

Well, Python has the following decision and repetition structures:

- If...else statement(s)
- For Loop
- While Loop
- Break and Continue
- Pass

Let's jump in and get started.

#1: If...else

In Python, a simplest if ... statement has the following syntax:

If Boolean expression

    Statements

It's important to note that the body of the Python's if ... else statement is always specified by the indentation. It should begin with an indentation where the first un-indented line marks the end of the statement. The non-zero values are interpreted as **true** while none and 0 are always interpreted as **false**.

Here's an example of code that tests if the average score is greater than or equal to 80 and displays grade "A".

```
number = float(input("Type any number from the Keyboard: "))

if number > 0:

        print ("The number you have entered is positive number")

        print ("This is how the if statement works")
```

The if ... else statement can only be executed when the Boolean expression is true. Otherwise, the statement will be skipped. In some cases, if statement can be followed by an else statement that is optional. When there's optional if ... else statement, the optional statement will be executed only when the Boolean expression returns false. Here's the syntax:

```
If Boolean expression:

  Python Statements

Else:

  Python statements
```

In this case, the if... else statement will evaluate the Boolean expression and execute its body statements only when test condition is True. But if the Boolean condition is False, then the body of else will be executed. Note that indentation is being used to separate the blocks. Here's an example:

```
number = float(input("Type any number from the Keyboard: "))
if number > 0:

        print ("The number you have entered is positive number")
else:

        print ("The number you have entered is a negative number")
```

Python can also allow you to specify multiple expressions. In this case, you'll use the *elif* which is synonymous with else if nested statements in other programming languages. In this case, if the Boolean condition is False, the program checks the Boolean condition of the next elif block and the process goes on. It's essential to note that an if block can contain only one else block. However, it can have several elif blocks.

Here's an example of Python code demonstrating the elif:

```
number = float(input("Type any number from the Keyboard: "))
if number > 0:

        print ("The number you have entered is positive number")
elif number == 0:

        print("The number you've entered is Zero"):
else:

        print ("The number you have entered is a negative number")
```

Ready for another test? Open the Shell and copy the Python code below, making sure to include every letter and symbol, correctly. When you're done, press the Enter key to execute the file.

Python Code:

```
import sys
def main ():
main()
{
if average>=70:
        grade="A."
elif average>=60:
        grade=" B."
elif average>=50:
        grade=" C."
elif average>=40:
        grade=" D."
else:
grade=" F."
}
```

#2: For Loop

The for loop in Python iterates over a sequence which may include Python's data types; list, tuple, string. It may also iterate any other objects that you define in Python. Here's the syntax for the for loop:

```
for val in sequence:
    Python statement(s)
```

In this case, *val* refers to the variable which takes the value of the item contained in the sequence for each iterative process. The looping process will continue so long as the last item in the sequence hasn't been reached. Note that the body of for loop is separated from the rest of the Python code using indentation.

Here's an example of a Python code that demonstrates how sum of all numbers stored in a list can be obtained:

```
mynumbers = [100,200,300,400,500,600,700,800,900,1000]
sum = 0
for val in numbers:
    sum = sum+val
print ("The sum of 10 numbers in your list is", sum)
```

#3: While Loop

In Python, the while loop iterates over a block of program statements as long as the Boolean expression—which is a condition—is true. You'll use this loop if you don't know the number of time to iterative in advance. Here's syntax of the Python's while Loop:

```
while Boolean expression:
    Program statements
```

In the above syntax, the Boolean expression is evaluated first. The program statements in the body of the loop can only be executed if the Boolean expression is true. After the first iteration, the Boolean expression is checked again. This process will continue until the Boolean expression evaluates to False.

Here's an example of a Python code that prompts a user to enter n numbers from the Keyboard and sums them:

```
n = int (input ("Enter the value of n :"))

total = 0

index = 1

while index <= n:

    sum = total+ index

    index = index+1

print ("The sum of n numbers is: ", total)
```

#4: Break and Continue

There are some instances when you just want to terminate the current iteration—whether in for loops or while loops—or even the whole loop without evaluating the Boolean expression. In this case, the break and continue statements changes the flow of a normal loop in Python.

When you break a loop using the break statement, the control of the program will flow to the program statement that is after the body of the loop. However, if the statement is inside a nested loop, then the break statement will terminate the innermost loop. Here's the syntax for break statement:

```
break
```

Here's an example of code that uses the break statement in Python:

```
for val in "Ultimate Beginner's Guide to Python":
    if val == "e":
        break
    print(val)
print("The program has reached the end of the string")
```

What about the continue statement?

Well, the continue statement skips the rest of the code that's inside a loop for the current iteration only. In this case, the loop will not terminate. It will continue with the next iterative process instruction. The syntax for continue is:

```
continue
```

Here's an example of code that uses the continue statement in Python:

```
for val in "Ultimate Beginner's Guide to Python":
    if val == "e":
        continue
    print(val)
print("The program has reached the end of the string")
```

#5: Pass

The pass statement in Python is treated as a null statement. I know you're now asking yourself, "Why shouldn't I just use comments instead of a pass?"

Well, the difference between a comment and pass statement is that while the Python interpreter ignores comments, the pass statements has to be executed. However, nothing happens when the pass statement is executed. Put simply; the pass statement acts as a placeholder. For instance, you may have a loop that you haven't implemented, but you'd like to implement it in future, then you can use the pass statement.

Here's an example:

```
def function(args):
    pass
class Bank:
    pass
```

There you have it. Understanding how to use decision and repetition structures in Python will help you to specify the program flow and use your variables efficiently.

Chapter 6: Python Functions

This chapter discusses the Python functions. By the end of the chapter, you should be in a position to define and use Python functions. But first, let's define functions and their significance in Python programming.

A function—also referred to as procedures or even subroutines in other programming languages—is simply a section of the program that's independent of the main program. It helps to map zero or even more input arguments. The primary objective of specifying a function in code is to assist group program statements that can perform related tasks.

Why are functions essential in Python programs?

Well, functions will provide very useful insights when you want to develop constructs which help you organize your code. A program that lacks functions has so many lines of codes that may be confusing. Debugging such programs isn't easy. Furthermore, having functions in your code makes your code reusable.

Syntax of Python Functions

Here's the syntax for specifying function in Python:

```
def name_of_the_function (parameters):

    Program statement(s)
```

As you can see from the syntax above, Python functions have the following parts:

- They begin with the keyword "**def**" that marks the beginning of a function header.
- The keyword "def" is followed by the name of the function you're creating. The name of the function must follow the conventional rules of naming identifiers.
- Arguments or parameters that are passed to the function (they are enclosed in brackets). They are optional.
- A colon (:) that marks the end of the function header.
- One or more valid python program statements which forms the function body.
- An optional return statement that returns a value from the function.

Here's an example of how you can specify a function in Python:

```
def greetings(myname):
    print("Hi! " "+myname + ". Good evening! How has been your day?")
```

How to call a function

If you've defined a function, you can call it from any other function, program or even the Python shell. For you to call a function, you simply type the name of the function with appropriate parameters. Here's an example of a Python code that calls the function called "greeting" which we had earlier designed:

```
greeting("Peter Namisiko")
```

Here's is the output of the program:

```
Hi! Peter Namisiko. Good evening! How has been your day?
```

Sometimes, you may want to exit the function and return to the place in the code from where it was called from. The return statement will help you to exit a function and go back to program location where the function was called from. Here's the syntax of the return statement:

```
return [expression_list]
```

The return statement can contain expressions—which will be evaluated—to find the value to be returned. If there is no expression in the statement, then the function returns None object. Here's an example of such a code:

```
def absolute_value_of_a_number(number):
    if number >= 0:
        return number
    else:
        return -number
print(absolute_value_of_a_number(100))
print(absolute_value_of_a_number (-300))
```

Types of Functions

There are two types of function in Python:

- Built-in functions
- User-defined functions

Let's dive in and find out the differences between these two types of functions.

#1: Built-in functions

These are functions that are already built into the Python. For instance, functions such as print (), input (), etc.—which we have been using so far—are examples of Python built-in functions. Other examples of built-in functions are:

#2: User-defined functions

These are functions that are specified by users. User defined functions are important because of the following reasons:

- They can help you to break down a large program into small segments which make your program easier to understand and debug.
- They can help you include codes that you can only execute when it's necessary if the codes are repeated.
- If you're working on a large project, user-defined functions can help you to divide the workload by into different functions.

That's it. By adhering to rules of using Python functions—which we've learned in this chapter—you'll be fast-tracking your way to becoming a professional Python programmer!

Chapter 7: Introduction to Python's GUI Programming

What we've discussed so far about Python programming is writing text-only programs that can be executed on Python's command-line interface. However, if you'd like to develop a large software system within a shorter time, then text-only programs can't provide you that functionality.

You need a GUI (Graphical User Interface) environment to help you not only fast-track the development of your programs, but also provide you with an easy-to-use interface which makes your code easier to understand and debug. But I know you're wondering, "What exactly is GUI programming?"

Well, GUI programming is just like any other type of programming that you've interacted with before. For instance, you can use the sequences, looping, and branching—just like the text programming. However, in GUI programming, you'll be using a toolkit that must adhere to the patterns of the program as laid down by the toolkit vendor.

Python is best suited for rapid application development of programs on cross-platform systems which includes the desktop GUI apps. But not all the toolkits are the same. Each toolkit has its own API and therefore, there are design rules a programmer has to learn before he/she can use that toolkit.

Therefore, some decisions have to be made regarding the right Python toolkit for rapid application development of programs. Before we explore various Python toolkits, it's important to learn factors that may affect the choice of a particular toolkit.

Factors that influence the choice of Python Toolkit

Here are factors that can influence the selection of a particular toolkit:

#1: Does it support theming?

Themes can be viewed as a collection of images and icons which provide a consistent look and feel of a programming interface. Therefore, before you decide on which toolkit you'd like to use for the rapid development of your Python software, you've to look for the best toolkit that has better images and icons.

#2: The number of widgets available in the toolkit

A toolkit with more widgets—including the native ones—will provide a better interface to interact with during the development of an application.

#3: Does the toolkit provide cross-platform environment features?

If you want to change the development of an application from one platform—say Windows OS platform to Linux OS platform—then you should have a toolkit that has similar features on both platforms.

#4: Which version of Python does the Toolkit Support?

Knowing which version of Python the toolkit supports will help you to know the version of Python to install.

Examples of Python Toolkits

Here are examples of Python toolkits—and their features—that can provide GUI programming to fast-track the development of your programs:

#1: TkInter

TkInter is one of the oldest Python GUI that has been distributed with Python since the inception of the language. It's a cross-platform toolkit with Python API—which can work with all the

Python versions. Besides being stable and reliable, it's also easy to learn and is object oriented. However, the toolkit has limited support for theming.

#2: wxPython

It's a cross-platform GUI toolkit that has several sets of widgets which are native and can be used on Windows, Linux, and OS X systems. It also has a large user base. However, it's not included as part of Python. However, its documentation is atrocious and its API unpleasant to most users.

#3: pyGTK/pyGobject

It is a cross-platform widget toolkit that's based on the GTK+--GUI toolkit that was developed initially for GIMP. The pyGobject is a new revision of pyGTK which uses the GObject introspection and other features of GTK3. These toolkits can be used on both Windows and Linux systems. They have excellent documentation and friendly GUI, which appeals to most programmers.